THE LIGHT OF LOVE

INSPIRATIONAL POETRY FOR VALENTINES AND OTHER LOVERS

TWELVE POEMS TO INSPIRE GIFT BOOK SERIES
BOOK THREE

ORNA ROSS

Copyright © 2023 Orna Ross
The authors's moral rights have been asserted.
All rights reserved.

Font Publications is the publishing imprint for Orna Ross's fiction and poetry, the Go Creative! books and planners and Alliance of Independent Authors publishing guides.
All Enquiries: sarah@ornaross.com

* * *

THE LIGHT OF LOVE
Inspirational Poetry for Valentines and Other Lovers
E-Book: 978-1-909888-72-2
Paperback: 978-1-909888-73-9
Large Print: 978-1-909888-61-6
Hardback: 978-1-909888-62-3
Audiobook: 978-1-909888-74-6

PRAISE FOR ORNA ROSS

"Highly ambitious, engaging and evocative."

— SUNDAY INDEPENDENT

"Breathtakingly powerful phrases pepper the pages, little puffs of magic whose brilliance takes you by surprise."

— DEBBIE YOUNG, BEST SELLING AUTHOR OF BEST MURDER IN SHOW

"Orna Ross has certainly rekindled my joy in celebrating the natural world, landscapes, the sacred, and the individual, in refreshing the soul with her ability to craft words and poetic lines that sing, dance and tell a story of hope and wonderment."

— MALA NAIDOO, GOODREADS REVIEWER

"[Ross's poetry] is not programmatic in any way, but its intentionality both provides space for, and evokes imagery of those everyday mundane glimpses of profound beauty that are typically overlooked, over-run, and driven past."

— KEN GOUDSWARD, GOODREADS REVIEWER

"One will keep [this poetry series] close, perhaps by the bedside, for dipping and delighting and drawing calm, joy and solace in our hectic world where allowing 'what is' can be a challenge."

— CHRISTINE MILLER, GOODREADS REVIEWER

"Spot-on brilliant. Orna Ross was so very gentle and clear in helping the reader understand mindfulness and what one can accomplish by staying in the moment."

— BOB JACKSON, GOODREADS REVIEWER

For Ross and Ben

"Love makes your soul crawl out from its hiding place."

— ZORA NEALE HURSTON

CONTENTS

Twelve Poems to Inspire: Gift Book Series   xi

THE LIGHT OF LOVE

Part I
DAWN

The Light of Love	5
Hush	9
On Borrowed Time	12

Part II
DAYLIGHT

Love Hurts?	17
The Rings of Our Being	21
Fire	26

Part III
TWILIGHT

The Next Birth	31
Long Love	35
Candy Darling on Her Deathbed	38

Part IV
NIGHTLIGHT

Rekindling   45
Into Ease   48
The Only Answer   51

Let's Keep in Touch   55

Award Winning Inspirational Poetry   57
Acknowledgments   59
About The Poet   61

TWELVE POEMS TO INSPIRE: GIFT BOOK SERIES

The Light of Love is the third book in the *Twelve Poems to Inspire Gift Book* series, poetry gift books for every occasion. Each poem is illustrated with an AI image generated by lines from the poem. A copy of the book, particularly a signed copy, makes a perfect gift on Valentine's Day, or anytime you want to celebrate love.

Saint Valentine is said to have been a Christian martyr, thought to have lived in the 3rd century AD, though Christianity recognizes at least three different martyred saints named Valentine or Valentinus, and there is also at least one registered female Saint Valentina. Though the name remains on the list of officially recognized saints, the Roman Catholic Church discontinued Valentine's veneration in 1969, just as the 14th February secular celebration began to take off.

In these poems (for valentines and other lovers), I explore some of the ways in which love illuminates our lives, from the first flutter of attraction, to the tenderness of a long-term bond, from the binding ties of family to the cosmic consolation of spiritual love.

We begin life knowing love as something we receive. No matter how deprived our start, if we've survived, we were shown some love by someone. Then, somewhere along the line, we have to grow up emotionally and learn that love is really about what we give. The lesson is rarely easy.

No heart escapes blood's surges, whereby the flow towards joy always ebbs into the ache of loss. Systole, diastole. Love hurts, and our hurt cries out, as we blame love itself for the pride and passions we bring to it, or for somebody else's bad behavior. Yet love—true love, real love—is the one thing that will never hurt us. It is the great healer, the great connector.

It is love that has brought you here, to this book, this intimate meeting of minds in words and it is love that will take you beyond any social difference or distancing, beyond color, class, and any other creed the human mind likes to construct.

This book is dedicated not to my life-long love, who has inspired so many of these poems, but to my son and soon to be son-in-law. It's not long since, in our country, a love like theirs was forbidden by law and custom. How foolish all that seems now, but there are still so many places where people are killed, imprisoned and tortured for loving. As a species, we still have a lot of emotional growing to do.

Love will take us there. Love moves us on, makes us better, opens every good thing up. Each day, this irresistible force works its miraculous magic on the human family, forever bringing us together, forever offering each one of us its purity and goodness.

We, being only human, cannot always be pure and good but the miracle is: as soon as we can find love within, then we are.

And the essence of the miracle is: we always can. As soon as we open to it, let go of our hurts and angers, our notions and opinions, love will dry our eyes and quiet our fears. Love will shine through us and transform us.

It is our answer to nothing less than everything.

Le grá,
Orna

THE LIGHT OF LOVE

TWELVE POEMS TO INSPIRE GIFT BOOK SERIES: BOOK III

PART I
DAWN

THE LIGHT OF LOVE

ORNA ROSS

THE LIGHT OF LOVE

The moon tonight is tilted
towards Earth, and waxing.
An edge of white lights its lower side,
and it admires its own lustre
in the seawater mirror
which is swooning in waves
at the sight.

Together, they remind me of you.
The tidal core of you, emerging
from beyond your story, washing up
on the the shore of us, bringing
the light offering of your secret self,
the dark offering of your sacred self,
all silvered where the heart quails,
waxing and waning.

The body too sometimes hesitates.
And oh, the wavering mind
and its need to be right.
But the moon remembers
how we have floated on the night.

Here, we know yet the bruises we carry,
inherited hurts given to us by the world
on entry, our need to take them out for,

and sometimes on, each other. But
then again, how would love know
what to do with itself
without the illumination
of fight and fright?

So we own them, together.
Accept their gifts and graspings,
hold them in night's still sight,
feel the flaxen moon's reminder,
as we watch it kiss the silken
darkness all along its edge of light.

HUSH

HUSH

Hush. Don't speak it aloud, beloved,
the crowd will sneer.
Though we know what we hold,
whisper it only to the wise
and to me, made wise by our love.
Take my hand from your mouth,
see, fade yours into mine.
Feel me here. And here.
Dying. Dying for you.

Murmur wings of gossamer steel
into being. Wave their wind
through the turnings of time.
Oh yes, we will ruffle the shrouds,
we will upend the season's
parading if we only allow.
Come. Cup our breath,
our shared life,
two made one, into none.
Shade us out. Sigh it sheer.

*　*　*

ON BORROWED TIME

THE LIGHT OF LOVE

PART II
DAYLIGHT

LOVE HURTS?

ORNA ROSS

LOVE HURTS

Love hurts, they say.
I say, no way.
The only thing that never hurts
is love.

Lust festers,
envy bites.
Loss skewers,
rejection spikes.
Passion burns,
craving seethes.
Romance dazzles,
lonesome bleeds.
Well yes, indeed.
But none of the above
is love.

Love helps,
love lights.
Love warms,
love rights.
Love soothes,
love feeds.
Love calms,
love heals.

Yes,
what will heal
the sting of pain,
and make your life
feel good again,
(again,
again,
and yet again),
is love.

Love hurts, they say.
I say no way.
The only thing that never hurts
is love.

* * *

THE RINGS OF OUR BEING

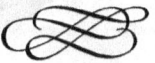

FOR CLARISSE AND BOBBY

THE LIGHT OF LOVE

THE RINGS OF OUR BEING

Commissioned by our family friend, Clarisse: a wedding poem in the style of seventh century Irish love poetry.

My love, and my hope,
from here will we go
into the wood,
down by the river,
scattering the dew
of this day.

There we'll see the trout
and the bulrushes,
the blackbird on its nest,
the little birds that are sweetest
singing in twos
from their branches.

I do not ask today
for your love as du
that not cling
and you'll not be
a strangulation.

I ask only to stand,
to sit and lie down with you
under the kindness of trees.

There will we meet
the shy deer,
and the buck calling.

When you trip,
I'll help you to your feet.
Will you wait for me,
when someday I run slow?

Let us be together
without having or holding
And may we never bring in
the idea of making
the other better.

I am not your task.
You are already complete.

Only let the rings
of your being
widen in mine,
mine in yours.

Then death
shall never devour us.

For as long as we live
will we thrive

down by the river
in the dew-dappled wood.

FIRE

THE LIGHT OF LOVE

FIRE

To carry a flame, you must burn.
And you do, with a dragon's fire roar
louder than a thousand engines igniting.

It keeps you throwing yourself
at the door of your own sky.
Kindling within and without,
burning down your barricades.
You won't stop until you answer
your own call, allow your own lighting,
fire yourself back into the infinite life,
the eternal blaze that consumes
everything in time but itself.
Succumb. Be sucked into the root,
its violet-blue heart. Flick back out
yellow tongues of flesh fired.

Melt the aureate air. Make liquid
brass of your blood. You hold the flame.
Already, you burn.

* **

PART III
TWILIGHT

THE NEXT BIRTH

THE LIGHT OF LOVE

THE NEXT BIRTH

The first birth came with mother's touch.
Skin shivering, lungs gulping,
life wakened me to feed and need
through years of trials and toys.
And then, just when I feared
I might drift away,
along came love, again —
it held me where I knew I should belong.

When bodies bare, we two in one combined,
each breath became yours and yours was
mine,
no day could ever be a day adrift
and all that came before us came as gift.
Once you loved me, as I loved you,
our young lives then began again, anew.

And so, in two renewed
we found new trials and toys.
Two children's need to feed arrived.
Their hearts upheld by mine inside
at first, and still outside they cleaved
until, one day, they seemed to slip away.
And then, just when we feared
our toils had been vain,
along came love, again

to hold us where we felt we each belonged.

When four lives in one family combined,
when their breath became ours as yours was
    mine,
no day could ever be a day of rift
and all that came before us came as gift.
Once four knew all loved one and three and two,
our melded lives began again, anew.

And so in shape renewed
we found new toys and trials,
more years of need and feed.
And if, at times, in cold despair we cry
along comes love, again
to hold us where we know we all belong.

When, spirits open, all in one combine,
in ways the sages know to be divine
when breath that's known as theirs
holds ours and yours and mine,
no day can ever be a day adrift
and all that comes before us comes as gift.
Once we know life loves us and we love too,
our life, right then, begins again, anew.

* * *

LONG LOVE

A SONNET

ORNA ROSS

THE LIGHT OF LOVE

LONG LOVE

We've been together for so long, my dear.
The world discounts us, thinking old means
void.

CANDY DARLING ON HER DEATHBED

THE LIGHT OF LOVE

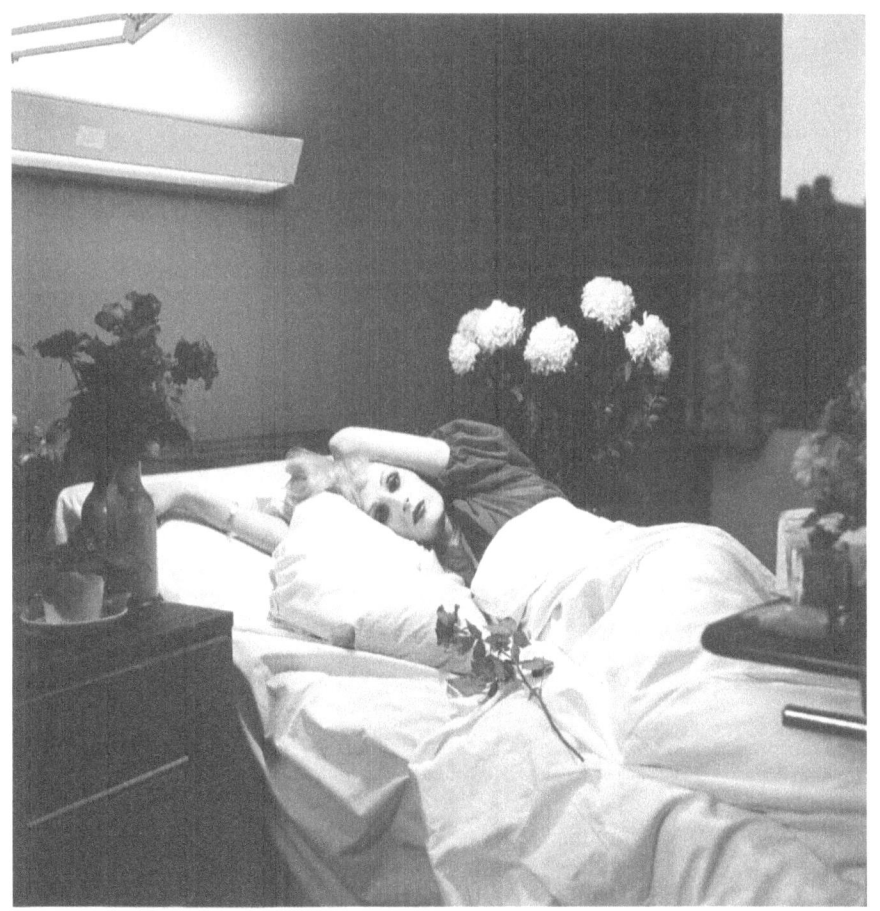

PeterHujarArchive.com

CANDY DARLING ON HER DEATHBED

On the table
in a vase by her bedside
six blooms, white
as the sheet she lies on
and the one folded
across her chest
lying in wait,
one day soon
to cover her face.

On that would-be shroud,
a single stem, cut,
its thorns and leaves
even its flower dark
as the curve
of Candy's eyes,
her lips, her ways.

In shades of night and light
she awaits the demise
of her days
and her designation,
dying as she has lived
since she ceased
to be a he.

THE LIGHT OF LOVE

Oh Candy.
Candy Darling.

* * *

PART IV
NIGHTLIGHT

REKINDLING

REKINDLING

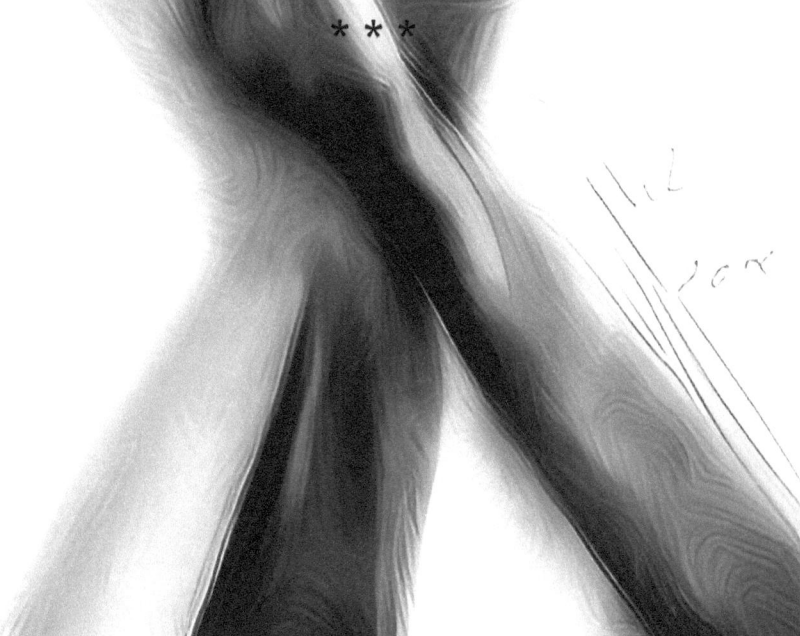

After long heartbreak,
hands and limbs are unlacing
ink-spattered veins, stencilled
vessels, old rents of paper skin torn
by words fierce felt, and senses
deep driven, now set to slumber
and forget. Light fingertips
are grazing against remembrances,
the fragile, scored terrain recalling
trembling innocence, ancient pining,
as quivering hands and limbs
are touching. Intertwining.

* * *

INTO EASE

THE LIGHT OF LOVE

INTO EASE

My darling, let's not sigh
to see day fade,
the earth receive the sun,
the light recede.

Let us, with sky and trees,
dim to dusk mood,
fall deep, and deep,
and deeper into ease.

When hands and head
and heart are brought to rest,
soft violet glows,
sweet silver starts to gleam.
Black darkness holds a place
for us, my love.
Come now. Let us lie down
in nightlight's dream.

THE ONLY ANSWER

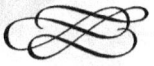

THE LIGHT OF LOVE

          stumble into life,
       another a   nt called me.

   u know tha we were invited
   the great n
       into visibility   ry forth
    a, for a tim
       form, as offering?

           eel how it feels
    wash out each other's wounds,
   mooth the sacred, secret salve
   into our skins, soothe the dazzle
   of what is said and done?

              ge of everything

* * *

LET'S KEEP IN TOUCH

Enjoyed the poems? Would you like more? If you're online, we have lots of ways to continue the poetic conversation.

UPDATES & BONUSES

My monthly email brings you my inspirational poetry news and ideas, discounted books, and other pen-friend presents. Follow the link below to become my poetry pen-friend and get a **free e-book**

OrnaRoss.com/Free-Poetry

PLEASE REVIEW THIS BOOK ONLINE

If you enjoyed this book, please give it a quick review online by visiting the link below and selecting the "Reviews" tab. Your review doesn't have to be long or detailed. A quick star rating and a sentence or two that helps others to understand the value of this book is all that's needed. I appreciate the support more than you know. *Go raibh maith agat!*

OrnaRoss.com/LightOfLove

BECOME A PATRON

For a small investment, you can become a direct patron of the arts! You make a small monthly payment to support my work and I send you a welcome gift, a poetry e-book each month and my poetry news. You can also opt in for more, at higher levels of support. More info: OrnaRoss.com/Poetry-Patrons

AWARD WINNING INSPIRATIONAL POETRY

Treat yourself to more poetry

Browse and buy more inspirational poetry books on my website: OrnaRoss.com/Poetry-Books

ACKNOWLEDGMENTS

My thanks to my publishing team: Sarah Begley, Kayleigh Brindley and Dan Parsons, who assist me in getting the words to my readers. To Jane Dixon-Smith for cover design of this book and the *Twelve Poems to Inspire Gift Book* series. To the #**IndiePoetryPlease** community on Instagram, thank you for reading, thank you for writing. To the creators of the AI art tool Dream by Wombo, app.wombo.art, which generates artwork from lines of the poems. To the Peter Hujar Archive for the portrait Candy Darling on her Deathbed, which inspired that poem. To Philip Lynch, first reader and frequent muse. And a special thanks to my poetry patrons. Your support and encouragement keeps the poems coming when other things threaten to take over. With a bow, thank you all. *Sonas libh go léir*.

x Orna

ABOUT THE POET

Orna Ross is an award-winning self-published novelist and poet, and founder of the Alliance of Independent Authors (ALLi). Enjoying book sales in 120+ countries worldwide, she has won several awards and her work for ALLi has seen her named "one of the 100 most influential people in publishing" (The Bookseller). Born in Waterford and raised in Wexford, in the south-east corner of Ireland, she now lives and works in London and St Leonard's-on-Sea, in the south-east corner of England.

Find out more at
OrnaRoss.com

- amazon.com/Orna-Ross/e/B001K86OBA
- goodreads.com/ornaross
- patreon.com/OrnaRoss

www.ingramcontent.com/pod-product-compliance
Lightning Source LLC
Chambersburg PA
CBHW020133130526
44590CB00040B/583